COOKIES TO CONTRACTS:
50 Ways to Public Speaking Intelligence

STEPHANIE SALASEK

First paperback edition December 2023

Cover art and illustrations by Graham Roumieu

Stephanie Salasek: Look Up Communications
www.stephaniesalasek.com

ISBN: 979-8-218-33816-9 (paperback edition)

To my dad—
the prop man at home,
in his classroom,
and on every stage.

TABLE OF CONTENTS

INTRODUCTION

With a mid-August birthday, I was one of the youngest in my kindergarten class. My height and weight, though, didn't fit my age. Throughout elementary school and junior high, I was taller and weighed more than my classmates. I recall my elementary P.E. teacher yelling, "Get moving, marshmallow!" as I tried to chug around the track, and my brother nicknamed me "Fatty Fiddle."

Throughout those years, I would lie in my twin bed with the white frame and pink chiffon cover gazing at the ceiling and dreaming about someone picking me for the recess kickball game or asking me to hang out on the monkey bars. My cup was filled a little when my second-grade teacher, Mrs. Ulin, delegated me to help the new student from South Korea with English, and when the principal, Mr. Dooley, started a four-square tournament and jump rope competition for those of us who weren't going to be picked for anything else.

What changed the game for me? Bringing cookies to school. Those cookies were my ticket to do the choosing. I got to select one classmate to pass out napkins and another one to pass out the treats. My mom was a home economics teacher, and I took nothing short of blue ribbon cookies every time. In my mind, I was popular for the day.

My clients are subject matter experts, organizational leaders, and faculty who need to be popular speakers for the day and manage the outcome at the conference and in front of stake-holders. They need to think about their audience like I thought about my classmates and do everything possible to surprise and delight them.

The basic recipe for public speaking success includes subject matter expertise, logical organization, and a great delivery all mixed together. *Cookies to Contracts: 50 Ways to Public Speaking Intelligence* is about taking care of the audience—the blue ribbon ingredient.

GATHER YOUR INGREDIENTS

(PREPARATION)

1

BREAK THE SCRIPT

When audience members take their seats, they expect what they've seen from other speakers: a greeting followed by lots of slides and a talking head. You need to "break the script" and give them more. Your goal is to exceed expectations—to surprise and delight the audience and leave them satisfied when you are finished speaking. You must be ingenious to keep your audience members intrigued and interested.

At the very least, beginning with an attention-getter that is not the title slide and does not contain "thank you for coming," is a good start. Keep your audience awake with minimum text slides, stories that bring soul to your data, book giveaways, and memorable moments. When technology betrays you, be ready to go with an activity that keeps the momentum going while you or your team fix the problem. Long waits for things to be fixed are attention killers. Don't forget about humor. Appropriate cartoon panels included in your slide deck, props that get a chuckle, and some self-deprecation are all winners. Your audience can only manage one emotion at a time—ecstatic and exuberant beat disappointed and disillusioned.

> **The secret to humor is surprise.**
>
> —Aristotle

"Breaking the script" is my mantra. I do this a lot in my personal and professional life. Years before I was dating my now-husband, I thought it would be fun to send a fictitious wedding announcement with a fake partner out for April Fool's Day. I may have been the most surprised when I received cards, money, and gifts in return. I don't want you to do anything this extreme in your presentation but move away from the status quo to improve the impact of your message. People remember what is novel and new.

2

WHAT'S IN A NAME?

Public speaking intelligence includes awareness and management of the whole experience for multiple audiences—from first contact to last contact. Learning names and correctly spelling and pronouncing them is a part of that intelligence.

Many of us have met someone and not committed their name to memory. You cross paths with them and kick yourself for not learning their name the first time. It's even worse if they remember your name and you can't reciprocate.

Don't let this be the case with your speaking work. Use any technique that works for you to remember names, including repeating it back when you meet someone the first time, creating an image in your mind, and writing it down when you can. All this effort on the front end will pay off for you.

During your presentation, you may call on people to participate. There

A person is more interested in their name than in all the other names on earth. So remember a person's name and call it easily, and you have paid a subtle and very effective compliment. But forget it or misspell it—and you have placed yourself at a sharp disadvantage...one of the simplest, most obvious, and most important ways of gaining goodwill is by remembering names and making people feel important—yet how many of us do it?

—*How to Win Friends and Influence People*, Dale Carnegie

will be times when there are name tags or name tents, but you can't count on this. After you ask someone's name, drill it into your memory so you can use it again during the same presentation or afterward when they thank you at the door. Remembering people's names means more to them than any expertise you bring.

When I was working in higher education, my director's name was Marc. He had a colleague in a different department who always spelled it "Mark." It didn't matter that these two sat in the same meetings and received the same emails many times a week. The colleague never took the time to learn the spelling, and it had a negative impact.

What's in
a Name?
ideas for me

3

SLIDE RIGHT THROUGH

I will not be adding designer to my skill set and I will not attempt design tips here. I have some advice for your slides, though, based on your audience's needs.

If there are brand colors associated with the audience you are speaking to, be careful to not use a competitor's colors. A distraction like this can be enough for some audience members to check out before your introduction. For the title slide, double-check you have the correct name of your presentation, the right organization or business name, and the accurate date. This may seem common sense, but I have seen more than a few presenters bring up the title slide and admit with embarrassment that they forgot to update the slide deck. Each audience is unique and special. It's the speaker's job to take care of the slide details, making each new audience a top priority.

> People don't remember what we think is important. They remember what they think is important.
>
> —*Everyone Communicates, Few Connect: What the Most Effective People Do Differently,* John Maxwell

I recommend that you do not number your slides. Numbers on your slides give the audience one more thing to think about. They may wonder if number 35 is close to the end or just getting started. Remove the distraction and eliminate the problem. If you need to use your organization's logo, don't use it on every slide. Put it on the title slide, two or three in the middle, and your last slide. The monotony of seeing the logo on every one dilutes the audience's experience.

I like to include images in my slides related to my audience when I speak. I will look for a picture of corporate headquarters for my business clients or a unique building on campus if I'm working with higher education clients. *Word of caution:* Make sure these images are current and not controversial. I send the images to my contact with the organization before I use them. It is one extra step that has saved me multiple times.

Slide Right Through ideas for me

4

PROPS AND 3D OBJECTS

What content do you remember from the last speaker you heard? There is a good chance you don't remember much. We forget quickly when we just listen and look at slides. We increase our retention when there is a relevant prop included. I'm not talking about stress balls or slapstick objects. I'm talking about enhancing your message with supportive visuals.

Think also about exaggerating your message with props that are extra big or extremely small. I have a pair of big Mickey Mouse gloves I put on when I want to stress a point and I use a miniature lectern and podium when I want to remind my public speaking participants that we stand *behind* a lectern and we stand *on* a podium. Props and objects that exaggerate can provide the benefit of an extra smile.

According to research by Michael Aun, an audience's retention is strongly tied to the use of visual aids. Following a speech given with no visual reinforcement, for instance, listeners retain only about 10 percent of information. If visuals such as slides, charts, props, etc., are added, retention rises to 60 percent.

—*The Toastmasters International Guide to Successful Speaking*, Jeff Slutsky and Michael Aun

I learned about props at a young age. My dad, a vocational agriculture teacher, used props in the classroom, school board meetings, and even church. He understood that people would recall the prop first and then remember the message. I likely slid under the pew out of embarrassment when he led our Percheron draft horse down the aisle with a saddlebag to kick off the annual stewardship drive. Though I bet anybody who was there that day still remembers his message.

Props and
3D Objects
ideas for me

5

GIVE IT AWAY

Giveaways can surprise and engage your audience. You could have a drawing for a book or throw some candy out to get participation rolling at the start. Stress balls are easy to brand and equally easy to catch without injury.

If you have a small group, contact a local bakery and provide a decorated cookie with the organization's colors and logo on each one. Distribute these in individual containers so participants can take them home or back to their office.

> Candy is a small and inexpensive gift to your audience that can perk people up and let them know that you're thinking about their comfort.
>
> —Lisa Braithwaite, Speak Schmeak blog

Having books on hand is a good idea for crisis recovery, too. You might give one to the audience member who unknowingly sat under a drip in the ceiling, or who grabbed the disposable coffee cup with a leak. Public speaking is like customer service in many ways; people forgive problems when the speaker or provider cares and helps them smile again.

I have a lot of fun giving things away after the audience has left when I head to my car. I hand extra cookies to people working in their offices and to staff I pass on my way out the door. They have no idea who I am, but a sweet surprise for them always makes my day.

Give it Away
ideas for me

6

BAGS, BOXES, AND BAGGAGE

Try to keep it tidy. I'm talking about how you pack your materials, including your computer, props, giveaways, and more. The audience is watching you. If a speaker brings in a lot of clutter that they have to rummage through to find things, it may give the impression of being disorganized and sloppy, which creates a challenge before you even begin to speak.

In addition, try to keep your car clean, even if you park in the back of the business or conference center. There's a good chance one of the participants will come out to help you carry things in or assist with your departure at the end.

> You don't get a second chance to make a first impression. In spite of the congeniality of many professional gatherings, judgments are being made and impressions formed all the time.
>
> —James Uleman, PhD, a psychology professor at New York University and researcher on impression management

I recommend plastic stacking crates for transporting your materials. They look sharp and are easy to carry. Try to pack your computer or other bag neatly. Make sure you have anything you will use in the restroom (e.g., floss, brush, lipstick, etc.) in a small bag that is easy to access and doesn't scream, "I am off to the bathroom to make sure I don't have lettuce in my teeth!"

We live off a gravel road. I remember skipping the car wash once and arriving with dust all over my car. After my first trip inside with materials, the event planner asked if he could help with the next load. It all went well until he shut the trunk, turning his navy blue suit to gray. Try not to skip the car wash.

Bags, Boxes, and Baggage ideas for me

7

RUNNER

Select the event planner or a friendly participant to be your extra hands and legs throughout the program. Waiting for audience members to make their way to the stage for a prize or straining to hear a volunteer in the back row will steal the momentum from your presentation.

It is best to have a conversation with the runner before you begin. Check with them to make sure they are capable of moving around quickly during the program and are enthusiastic about helping. A handheld microphone that passed the pre-show sound check with charged batteries should be presented to the runner before you begin. Show them how to turn the microphone off to prevent feedback when it is not in use.

In addition to making deliveries of giveaways and providing the microphone to audience participants, give the runner permission to get your attention if people can't hear you or are uncomfortable with background noise or room temperature. A good runner will be your hero and save the day.

> You can tell when an audience has stopped listening to you during a presentation. Phones come out, and attendees surreptitiously text underneath the table. Instead of leaning forward and nodding along with your points, they begin slouching or tapping their feet. The more brazen may even start whispering to one another.
>
> —Dorie Clark, "What to Do When You're Losing Your Audience During a Presentation," *Harvard Business Review*

During a recent program, my runner exceeded his 10,000 daily steps in our hour together. He also had a great sense of humor, and I was able to tease him as he sprinted from delivering prizes to running the microphone. He elevated the whole experience for the audience.

Runner
ideas for me

8

MULLIGAN STEW

Mulligan Stew was a popular educational TV series when I was a kid (I know, sounds like an oxymoron). It was about eating nutritional food and taking care of yourself. We watched the show at school, and it was my first introduction outside the home to good health.

Speakers must take care of themselves. I do not know what your physical limitations are—but if you can, try to exercise most days. Eat what you know works best for you. Sleep and sleep well. I could keep going, but this is not a book about health and wellness. I can only tell you that professional presence and mental acuity take a hit without exercise, good nutrition, and sleep.

If you're on the road speaking, plan ahead for accommodations with a fitness center, if possible, and a flight that will get you to your destination the night before for quality rest. Instead of grabbing a donut at the meeting, get going early in the morning and eat a balanced breakfast. These sound like the basics, but how many people follow them as they should?

> Regular exercise and a balanced diet increase energy levels and cognitive function. These factors directly impact your ability to engage an audience and stay mentally sharp while speaking.
>
> —Seriah Sargenton, Riyah Speaks blog

Mulligan Stew will stick in my mind forever because it was meaningful and memorable. I am most meaningful and memorable as a speaker when I take care of myself and can give 100%.

Mulligan Stew ideas for me

9

MOVE IT!

Moving with purpose when you speak requires planning and practice. Each venue will be different. Will your audience be sitting in chairs lecture-style, or around a boardroom table, or maybe in pods? Be sure you know the room layout and try to practice in the space before the event, if possible.

In the beginning stages of practice, you may need to make notes for yourself that say, "Move now." The easy plan is to move when you change to the next main point or move when you transition from the introduction to the body and finally to the conclusion. You don't want it to seem erratic or like a major event.

Speakers who move purposefully—not swaying or pacing—keep the audience engaged. You can move from one side of the room to the other in front and move toward and away from the audience if it's lecture-style. Each layout provides different options (e.g., open horseshoe, stadium seating, small group, etc.). Keep your eyes on the audience, and don't lose momentum. Moving will also help you, the speaker, relax if you have anxiety that needs to escape.

Think about the last tennis match you saw. Think about a dog running around in a park. We have to follow moving objects. It's an instinct. And we definitely follow moving objects on the horizon. This is what you are when you move horizontally on stage. You're a moving object on the horizon. And they just have to follow. When they follow your movements, the level of attention automatically goes up. It's that simple.

—Florian Mueck, Public Speaking Consultant

I move quite a bit in my programs. I like to make sure the back of the room is as much a part of the program as the front of the room. I get into trouble sometimes if I put my clicker down up front and need it again 40 rows away. Rather than run up there, I recruit a front-row audience member to grab the clicker and advance to the next slide. This gets the job done, often with a laugh.

10

I SCRATCH MY EAR?

You won't know what you look like and sound like in front of an audience until you record videos of yourself. If word gets around, I might be out of business, but video is the No. 1 coach out there.

When you watch yourself and see what your audience sees, and hear what your audience hears, you will be surprised. Your voice will sound different. You may not know you scratch your ear when you are searching for a word or that you stand on one foot while trying to explain a complicated graph. A coach or a colleague can tell you these things, but it hits home when you see it yourself.

The purpose of video recording is to give you control. Someone may have told you that you look like you are stuck in cement when you speak, but until you see yourself standing in one place—you may think others are highly critical. "Steady pitch" (aka monotone) is not a compliment for a public speaker. When you hear yourself on a recording, you can decide if you need to work on some voice modulation before your next presentation.

> Recording yourself on video—and then watching yourself—is the quickest, surest, most fool-proof way to improve your public speaking skills. I guarantee that in a matter of minutes, you'll see exactly what you need to fix. And you'll fix it immediately. It's far more effective than practicing in front of other people.
>
> —Claire Lew, "Got a Big Presentation Coming Up? This is the Most Effective Way to Improve Your Public Speaking," *Inc.*

I encourage my clients and workshop participants to get a video of themselves before they start to improve their public speaking skills. Much like a weight loss program, the before and after visuals validate our work and accomplishments.

11

WHICH AUDIENCE?

Public speaking isn't like putting on a theatrical performance for one audience. Each email, phone call, and virtual and in-person visit includes an audience. When you arrive to speak, someone will most likely greet you. This person is part of your audience and will spread the word about your attitude and demeanor even before you find the room. Tech support? Put your best foot forward. They can change the trajectory of your presentation to make you the star or the reason people leave early. Go out of your way to treat each audience with respect and kindness.

Be mindful that your presentation for the listening audience isn't over when you show your last slide or answer the final question. There will be audience members who want to visit with you in person, and there will be participants who write down your contact information and send you an email after the event. Be present for those in-person conversations and follow up within 24 hours for the emails. Each audience deserves the best.

Jody Urquhart, a keynote motivational speaker, observed the speaker before her on a program throw a fit behind the scenes when his expectations for technology and resources didn't meet his needs: "The motivational speaker for the HR conference was fantastic on stage. It's too bad that he left the wrong impression off-stage. It's not good business or good manners, and those who select guest speakers are looking for the total package."

One of my favorite parts of speaking is visiting with the team wrapping cords and stacking chairs at the end. These are the people who have done the hard work. A thank you and a gift card can be the surprise that makes their day.

12

DID THEY CRY?

When we prepare a presentation, gather all our stuff, put ourselves together, and arrive at the event, we believe everyone got out of bed to sit and listen to us. I can assure you that they did not.

Good speakers are aware that each audience member is in a unique state of mind emotionally and mentally. If we asked everyone present to share the last 24 hours of their life, we would take a seat and give them all a break.

Someone received news about a biopsy. Another got notice of a lay-off. The gentleman nodding off may have been up all night with an elderly parent, and the woman checking her phone may be waiting to hear if her

> We all crave connection. True connection requires respect and empathy—a recognition that we are all human, we all have our highs and lows and we are all doing our best. If we can walk into a room with that attitude, our chances of walking out with an objective met, a successful outcome, or a partnership forged are that much stronger.
>
> —Dean Brenner, "Embracing The Human: Using Empathy To Connect With An Audience," *Forbes*

daughter got through rush hour with a low tire. Assume the best and give your best. Never call anyone out or show disappointment.

I visited my dad at the University of Iowa Hospital & Clinics on a chilly fall day. When I said "goodbye," I knew he didn't have long to live, and soon I would be sharing my final farewell. I headed back toward Iowa State and stopped at an intersection in a small town. A man in a truck stopped on the north side of the intersection and then started gesturing and yelling at me. It took me a moment, but I soon realized it was a two-way stop, and I didn't have a stop sign. I hit the gas and went on my way. I wondered as I drove down the highway if that man would have yelled at me if he knew I just left my life hero in a hospital close to death. I never forget this story when I speak and think about what my audience may have been through before they arrived.

Did They Cry?
ideas for me

13

WHAT HAPPENED BEFORE YOU?

Take time to catch up with the local and national news on the day you speak. Audience members may be chatting about what's happening and there may be something that impacts your message.

If there are programs before you on the agenda, check with the event planner to see if you can attend. Audience members want you to be authentic and empathetic. If you are listening to the message they are hearing, you can incorporate bits into your presentation and ensure you don't repeat or contradict something. When it's your turn, mentioning the name and a specific point from a previous speaker goes a long way with everyone involved, too.

> Sir Ken Robinson created a genuine connection during his 2006 TED Talk by opening with compliments for the speakers who presented before him. His talk stands as the most popular TED Talk of all time.

Was it too hot in your room when the participants arrived? Did everything go smoothly with catering? Is the weather going to impact flights? You need to answer these questions for yourself to be the most effective. It's hard to listen when you are too hot or too cold, hungry, or worried about a timely, safe trip home. By addressing and being aware of these and other possible issues, you can make adjustments to your program and remove some distractions.

I remember speaking to a group of college students in an early morning class a few years ago. I didn't watch the news or check social media before I arrived to learn that some of these students were involved in a late-night campus protest the day before. These students were in their seats physically but somewhere else emotionally. I would have presented with a heightened awareness and sensitivity if I had learned about this before I spoke.

14

SOUND AND STAGE CHECK

You are scheduled to speak at 1 p.m. The sound and stage check are at 10 a.m. You will be there.

First, you need to select the best microphone if there are options. If a headset is available, take it. Second in line is a lapel microphone, and the third best option is a handheld microphone. The headset will pick up your voice no matter which way you turn. The lapel only works best when your head aligns with the physical microphone on your upper body. The handheld microphone may make your rock star dreams come true, but you are apt to misplace it, drop it, or swallow it (OK, you won't, but you may hold it way too close to your mouth for the audience to understand what you're saying). Second, you need to work with your event planner and the sound technician (if available) to walk to every area of the room to test volume and feedback.

> Why should you use a microphone? It will mean less strain for you; it allows for more expression to come across when you speak, and it is easier for your audience.
>
> —Simply Amazing Training

You noticed that I listed "stage check," too. It's your chance to see where you can move around in the space and not be blocked by a pillar or blinded by the projector light. You may decide to stay on the stage throughout your presentation, or you might want to move down or up to connect at eye level with the audience if it's an option.

Role-playing all of this at 10 a.m. beats learning at 12:55 p.m. that you have an immovable lectern microphone and you are stuck standing in one place.

I spoke to a group of about 5,000 students and chose the lapel microphone rather than the headset right before the event. When I finished and headed toward the event planner with a "that was pretty good" smile, she let me know there wasn't any sound on the right side of the auditorium. The lapel microphone was weak, only picking up my voice when I spoke directly into it.

Sound and Stage Check ideas for me

15

TECHNOLOGY BUST

Prepare for it all. It could be the internet, your computer, or maybe the projector that doesn't cooperate. There's a good chance it will not be all three of them at the same time, so you need to have an alternative plan for each one.

Always have your slides available from multiple places. Save them on your desktop, on a flash drive, in the cloud, and send them to the event planner. If your computer isn't working, you have three backup plans ready to go.

Print each slide on its own sheet of paper in full color. If you're presenting virtually, but the slide show isn't showing up, you can hold each sheet up for the camera. If you're in person, and the projector isn't working, the copies can serve as mini posters and guide you. The event planner can also send the slides via email to participants, who can use their devices to view the deck during the talk.

And finally, the internet. Keep internet use during your presentation to a minimum. Different locations, speeds, and obsolete passwords can get you in trouble and bog you down.

> Keep calm and keep presenting! Whatever technology glitches you may face before or during a presentation, just maintain your composure and continue your speech. Having a few anecdotes up your sleeve can help, too. Take a deep breath and remember you've got this! YOU are the presenter AND the presentation.
>
> —The Prezenter LTD, a presentation agency

Props, stories, humor, expertise, eye contact, engagement, metaphors, analogies, and a clear "why" statement are a few things that don't require one bit of technology for a successful audience experience. Trust your practice and yourself, and you will make it work.

I try to model what I just shared and I preach it all the time to my clients. At a recent event, the computer was set, the internet was fast, and the projector was bright. Just as we got started, though, the lights went out and we sat in the dark. Never think you've planned for everything.

Technology Bust ideas for me

16

COME FOR DINNER

You may receive an invitation to join the audience for dinner or a reception prior to or after your presentation. You must decide if it is appropriate and will work with your schedule. Politely decline if you won't be attending, and strategically plan if you accept the offer.

Let's say that the cocktail hour starts at 5 p.m., dinner starts at 6 p.m., and the program begins at 7 p.m. I recommend you arrive close to 5:45 p.m. The speaker should not spend an hour drinking or socializing before the program. Dinner is a good time to meet people, and remember a few names to use when you speak. It is also an opportunity to learn more about the individuals attending and the organization they represent. It is not a time to chat about yourself.

> Fear of public speaking is one of the most common phobias... Symptoms can range from mild anxiety to a full-blown panic attack, and many people who are forced to face their fear will use alcohol to get through the experience. However, research has shown that despite having the ability to calm nerves, alcohol can impair a person's ability to deliver a quality speech.
>
> —The Arbor Behavioral Healthcare

Make sure you take a trip to the restroom before the program begins. You could have ketchup on your tie or spinach on your tooth. In addition, you may need to fix your name tag and freshen your breath.

If the reception and dinner will follow the speaking program, don't let down your guard. All public speaking etiquette rules still apply. Be careful not to hang out with just a few people who may be singing your praises, either. Circulate as much as possible and thank your audience.

I have watched too many speakers arrive when the bar opens and embarrass themselves when the program starts. I recommend you stick with only one beverage if you choose to drink. It's not Thanksgiving dinner, either. Eat light so you are ready to wow them on stage rather than drift away into a food coma.

Come for Dinner
ideas for me

17

DELETE DISTRACTIONS

A last-minute trip to the restroom before you speak is more about removing distractions than emptying your bladder (although that is important). It's a chance to check yourself in the mirror before your audience looks you over and finds something more interesting than your message.

Start with your hair and move to your shoes. It does not have to be "perfect," but you may be surprised to find a smear of toothpaste on your lip or an error occurring before sunrise with one blue and one black shoe. How about a necklace caught on your name tag or the drive-through coffee that still smells good on the front of your suit jacket? These are all easy to spot if you plan ahead and look yourself over from head to toe.

Princeton University psychologist Alex Todorov and student researcher Janine Willis published research in *Psychological Science* that found people respond intuitively to faces so rapidly that our reasoning minds may not have time to influence the reaction. Their studies found that a tenth of a second is all it takes to make a snap judgment of a stranger.

If there is something that can't be changed or improved when you take this final look, it is acceptable and appropriate to call it out quickly to your audience and move on. Better for the audience to know you are aware, than for them to feel badly and wonder why nobody told you about the problem.

Take heed if you eat anything from the buffet tables at your programs. I am still embarrassed about the time I ate the fresh blueberries and skipped the final restroom trip. I facilitated a half-day workshop before I knew there was a blueberry skin on my front top tooth. I wanted to be mad at the audience for not letting me know, but it was my fault for not following my advice—DO NOT SKIP THE RESTROOM!

Delete Distractions ideas for me

FOLLOW
THE RECIPE

(EXECUTION)

18

WHO ARE YOU?

Your audience is interested in your message, not a lengthy introduction from the emcee or yourself about your credentials. I understand a speaker needs to establish credibility, but you were presumably asked to speak because a group of people knew you were an expert. I bet, too, that your biography is in the program or you were well-advertised beforehand. There is no need to beat the drum any longer.

When introductions go on and on, as an audience member, I wonder how this is helping the speaker's purpose. If the audience doesn't fall asleep, they may be intimidated hearing your life story and wonder if they will even understand your message. The speaker needs to build a relationship from the beginning—lengthy introductions will not accomplish that connection.

> You do not need to narrate a speaker's entire life story. Intros that go on too long lose their impact. You want to simply set the speaker up for success, not do their job for them.
>
> —Adam Christing, a professional emcee

For one of my presentations, I made up a few things about myself to see how the audience would react as the emcee read my introduction. I said I was a social media influencer, I did a little time as a hedge fund manager, and that I was on my third book. When I walked onstage, I could tell my first impression didn't fit what they had just heard. I confessed to my fun, and we all had a good laugh. The energy in the room rose with some humor rather than a long list of facts.

Who Are You?
ideas for me

19

ATTENTION-GETTER

Look up, lock in on an audience member, and start strong with your attention-getter. The majority of presenters start with social gratitude (i.e., "thank you for coming") and idle chatter. Audience members use this time to check their phones and drift away in their minds. Your attention-getter without the filler comments will surprise them and make a connection from the start.

Researchers at The Catholic University in Washington, D.C., found that most people stopped paying attention to a speaker only 30 seconds into the speech.

You need to think of your attention-getter as the most important first impression. Possibilities include relevant stories, statistics, metaphors, analogies, testimonies, and much more. You should not use any notes or slide cues for this. Your audience will decide during this time if they will listen to the rest of your message.

I have started some of my emotional intelligence workshops through the years with the story of a classmate who wanted to get me on the freight scale at the end of our third-grade field trip to a local factory. This story elicits gasps from the audience and puts the audience in a position to hear more about emotional intelligence. Your goal is to draw them in and ignite interest. "Thank you for coming" does not do this.

Attention-Getter ideas for me

20

TELL ME WHY

Write down your "why" statement before you do anything else with your presentation. There must be a tagline for your audience. It's great that you have lots of cutting-edge research, data, and ideas, but what is the audience supposed to think or do after they listen to you?

Here are some examples:

> All organizations start with WHY, but only the great ones keep their WHY clear year after year.
>
> —*Start with Why: How Great Leaders Inspire Everyone to Take Action,* Simon Sinek

- Emotional intelligence is responsible for 58% of your work performance, so understanding emotional intelligence—and how to improve it—is critical for job success.
- Surveys show public speaking is a fear for about 75% of the population. Including public speaking skill programs in your company's professional development plan will benefit your employees and the bottom line.

If I'm in the audience and I hear either of these "why" statements, I know right from the start the focus of the message and the desired outcome. The "why" statement should immediately follow the attention-getter. This "why" serves as a road map for the presentation. All supporting material following the statement should validate and corroborate it.

Think of the number of times you listened to a speaker wrap up their presentation and wondered to yourself about the purpose and the goal. You should never have to wonder. The "why" statement should lead the charge and make it clear from the start.

Tell Me Why
ideas for me

21

ROAD MAP

As the subject matter expert, the information, ideas, and stories you share as a speaker are unique to you. The value you bring to the stage is lost, though, if you don't organize your message like a map and check in with your audience to keep them on the road. Audience members feel empowered when you let them know where you are taking them, and they appreciate you for it.

An **introduction** will include an attention-getter, a "why" purpose statement, and an overview of your main points.

In the **body** of your presentation, you will support the main points with facts, stories, testimonies, ideas, images, and much more.

A speech format is like a map. You are the driver when you deliver a speech, and the audience members are your passengers. They want to know where you are taking them, how long it will take to get there, and what they can expect to see along the way.

—Knowledge Impacts Speaking Success (KISS) Speaking

Finally, there will be a clear **conclusion** that includes a reminder of the main points and the purpose, followed by an ending note.

My first career was teaching ninth-grade speech in a small town in Iowa. My students heard my mantra over and over, "Tell them what you're going to tell them; tell them; and tell them what you told them." I have a former student, Paul, who still stays in touch and always finds a way to slip that mantra into our conversation. He shares it with me to poke a little fun, but he always admits that he uses it every time he speaks, and it works.

Road Map
ideas for me

22

MESSAGE CLEAR

The audience may be more interested in reading your body language than listening to what you say. Your first impression begins the moment you enter the room. The audience reads these non-verbal messages as they watch you wait during the introduction and when the video doesn't cue up for you at the right moment. Your posture, gestures, and facial expressions tell the truth of your message.

What face will you make when a participant interrupts you with a question after the emcee announced in the introduction to save questions for the end? How about when you watch someone leave early or look over and see someone asleep? It's easy to smile and nod when you think the audience is tuned in and on your team. It takes practice and discipline to show this same attitude when things aren't going as planned. Scowls and frowns will only hurt you and your message.

> Vanessa Van Edwards, who researches human behavior, communication, and the science of relationships, set out to study the factors separating viral TED Talks from other, less popular ones. She found that nonverbal behaviors have an outsized impact...viewers decide if they like a TED Talk within the first seven seconds...While you're interacting with the audience before a speech, Van Edwards advises having "visible hands," making eye contact with people as you walk by, relaxing your shoulders, and keeping your head and chest high.
>
> —Toastmasters International

I am typically cold if I'm not outside in scorching heat. My unconscious tendency is to cross my arms in front when speaking for a bit of extra warmth. This can create a barrier between the audience and me and communicate the wrong message, so I dress in layers and give the audience permission to remind me to "open up."

Message Clear
ideas for me

23

HOUSEKEEPING HUMOR

The speaker who tells the audience to move to the middle, silence their phones, and wait for the end to ask questions has three strikes against them. These are small and routine requests, but they can inconvenience the audience and remove a little perceived control.

My first advice is to have another individual manage the housekeeping work before you speak. Let the audience dislike someone else. If you are a one-person show and need to provide instructions, try using light humor. An image of an outhouse could bring a smile as you explain the restroom locations; your phone ringing and you accepting the call could be a subtle and surprising way to make the point to silence theirs; and finally, a prepped group in the front row asking question after question can prompt you to encourage the audience to wait until the end to ask questions.

Public speaking expert Adam Christing says the event planner or emcee should always make the announcements. This job is not for the keynote or main speaker.

I have had the opportunity to give hundreds of welcomes for programs and events. My style includes light humor and subtle satire. On those occasions when I had to say, "Please move to the middle if there is space and make room for more guests," I could feel the energy leave the room. I went from the fun opening act to the mean teacher.

Housekeeping Humor ideas for me

24

SOMEONE SPECIAL

Audience members have listened to and watched a lot of speakers throughout their lives. They have an idea of what's going to happen from the time they sit down, to when they sneer at their neighbor, and when they exit quickly at the end. Your job is to prove them wrong.

The actual presentation is just one small piece of your success. Work with the event planner ahead of time to find out if anyone has a work anniversary, birthday, or another possible reason for recognition.

Your technical support team is your best friend during your time on stage. Take a moment to acknowledge their work and have something for this individual or team, too. If something goes wrong with your audio and visual program while you are speaking and you lean on the support crew, make sure you recognize them immediately. No one wants to be taken for granted.

> The Mind Tools content team says celebrating a milestone can give us an amazing feeling. And it can be even better when someone else acknowledges these achievements.

I hope you took good notes when you were working with the event planner ahead of your presentation. When you write the thank you note, mention personal life tidbits they may have shared with you; these might be about children, grandchildren, pets, travel, etc. We all want to be listened to and validated. They won't forget that you didn't forget.

I have recognized more than a few individuals who had 45 or 50 years with a company or organization. With so much turnover and so many new employees, this long tenure is often a surprise for the group. I love to watch the humble employee come forward to the sound of co-workers' cheers and clapping.

Someone
Special
ideas for me

25

POWER OF THE VOICE

A steady voice doesn't cut it. We need to incorporate the range of options we have available. These include variety with pitch, rate, tone, and volume. You are working all the time as a speaker to keep your audience with you, and varying your vocal patterns is a tool you have to accomplish this.

Think of pitch like a piano keyboard, where you have a range to go higher and lower. Rate is your speed. There are times when you want to go faster and others when you slow down.

> Vocal variety is more than merely avoiding the dreaded monotone. It is, at its foundation, the life that you breathe into what you say and do onstage.
>
> —Toastmasters International

Emotion is the tone. You can say the same words but with many different emotions to communicate the message. And finally, there is volume. Speaking at the same level throughout your presentation lulls the audience to sleep. You can speak louder and softer as needed.

Many speakers forget about the power of the voice to surprise the audience and keep them interested. The best way to learn how you sound is to record audio of yourself. We sound much different inside our heads than we do to others.

I tend to speak at a fast rate. I know people can think much faster than I can speak, but when I make a conscious effort to slow down, I see them tune back into what I'm saying. I probably lean on the loud side, too, so I like to get very soft and surprise the audience. The audience works hard in the first couple of minutes to figure out my voice and how I use it. When I "break their script" with vocal changes, they stick with me and remember what I said.

Power of
the Voice
ideas for me

26

I SEE YOU

Eye contact is a public speaking skill you can work on wherever you go. Start practicing by looking people in the eyes for a count of three seconds. It may seem awkward at first, but with practice, it will be a new habit soon. Meetings are wonderful places to start.

Eye contact connects us to other human beings. When you look someone in the eyes, you communicate that you are present with them and interested in them. You may have been told to look at the back wall when you present or imagine the audience members naked. Neither of these ideas will build a relationship with your audience.

I encourage my clients to look out in silence just before they speak, lock eyes with an audience member, and begin

> If there is one simple thing you can do to enhance your impact as a presenter—persuade others to see things as you see them and make it more likely your audience will say yes to your idea—it is sustained, purposeful eye contact with one person at a time.
>
> —Sims Wyeth, "10 Reasons Eye Contact is Everything in Public Speaking," *Inc.*

their attention-getter. It is true that when you look at everyone, you look at no one, but when you look at someone, you look at everyone. The audience is paying attention to your eye contact and feels it for themselves, even when you are looking directly at another person.

I remember an engineering client who hated this part of presenting. He tried to argue that eye contact with the slides was just as good. I remember when I watched his first presentation after our work together. He used the 3-second rule for eye contact, starting with the farthest person on the left in the front row and working over one person at a time (still in the front row) to the farthest person on the right. He was thrilled when his presentation was over, and he did not have to face the second row. We added an encore coaching session to practice including the whole audience.

I See You
ideas for me

27

NO BARRIERS

Work to avoid the fourth wall. It's the fictional wall in a theater, which allows the audience to watch the action but not be a part of it. Speakers create a fourth wall when they stand behind the lectern or a table. You can put your notes (if you have any) on the lectern and your props on the table, but always leave yourself open to the audience. When you remove physical barriers, you remove the idea that you are separate.

Folding your arms in front of you or standing in the fig leaf position also creates a fourth wall. Practice keeping your arms to your side or at waist level. You can keep one hand occupied with a clicker if you have slides or with props when it's time.

Simply Speaking, a newsletter for speakers, suggests that standing behind a lectern makes you more vulnerable because you feel like it is you versus the audience, instead of being one with the audience.

Moving around through the audience is a way to remove barriers, too. You don't want to fly around so much that people lose track of you, but it's nice to move toward the middle, around the edges, and sneak to the back when possible. Audience members are more interested and engaged when you are physically closer.

Sunglasses give me the illusion that others can't see me in the car or walking across the street. I don't know what it is, but I think I'm incognito when I wear sunglasses. My clients associate the same idea with standing behind a lectern; it provides a pseudo shield and identity protection.

No Barriers ideas for me

28

I WILL BE THE JUDGE

You have likely heard speakers use some common phrases. I've listed a few below:

- "A funny story…"
- "I will wrap up shortly…"
- "Interesting facts…"
- "You all know this…"

These are all subjective comments and assumptions. The audience may not think the story is funny or the facts are interesting. Your idea of wrapping up shortly may be very different than my idea of wrapping up shortly.

Announcing, "You all know this," sets you up for failure. There will be audience members who may not know what you are referencing, and now they are embarrassed and distracted.

> The most important thing in communication is to hear what's not being said. Audiences talk back in silence, apprehension, dismissal, head shakes, head nods, and handclaps. If we fail to pay these any mind we will lose.
>
> —Myisha Cherry, "Don't Talk to Your Audience, Talk with Them," *Entrepreneur*

It is hard to eliminate all these subjective phrases from your presentations, but you can listen more to what you're saying and adjust your word choices for a better outcome.

I remember saying, "I know that everyone is freezing," immediately after my attention-getter during a presentation. I bet 90% of the room shook their heads to say no. That one line put a big dent in my momentum and relationship with the audience.

I Will Be
the Judge
ideas for me

29

TELL ME YOUR STORY

Stories are not a "nice to have," they are a "need to have" when it comes to good public speaking. When you share a relevant story, your audience hears you talking with them, not at them. They make a connection with you that keeps them engaged and interested.

When you find yourself sharing a story with a friend or family member, write that story down. Recall as many specific details as you can when you document it. Think about how this story might fit into a future presentation. You will appreciate a library to pull from when you get the call and need to use it.

Good storytellers use first-person stories. If I tell you something that happened to me, it will feel more realistic in your mind than something that happened to my neighbor or colleague. To

In their book *Made to Stick*, Chip and Dan Heath conduct an experiment with Stanford students, asking them to prepare a 1-minute speech on whether or not non-violent crime is a serious problem. On average, the students used 2.5 statistics in their speeches, while only one student in 10 told a story. When remembering the presentations 10 minutes later, only 5% of the audience could recall any individual statistic, but 63% could remember the stories.

construct a story for the audience, you should identify the characters, set the scene, and paint the picture. Follow this with the conflict or problem, and finally, resolve the story and connect it to your message. Practice many times over until you choose the words that are just right to recreate the experience for your audience.

My brother has written a few compilations of humorous and surprising situations based on his work as a veterinarian. In his book, *All My Patients Have Tales*, he shares an anecdote about his sister, who has an extreme fear of dogs and ran from an elderly beagle hobbling around the town square. I looked it up, and about 7-9% of the U.S. population has a specific phobia, like a fear of dogs, while about 75% fears public speaking. If you have anxiety about public speaking, you have a lot more company than I do.

Tell Me
Your Story
ideas for me

30

SENSORY SECRETS

Sight, sound, smell, taste, and touch can be sensory secrets for your presentation. When you tell stories and provide information with flat words and text-heavy slides, your audience will either fall asleep or fill in the senses from their perspective and rewrite the message.

Consider this story, told in two different ways:

> When you use multiple senses (sight, smell, taste, touch, and hearing) to encode a memory, you increase your ability to encode the memory for later retrieval.
>
> —Brian Sullivan, co-founder of Big Design Conference

- **Example 1:** I learned to bake from my mom at a young age. She would stand right with me and help me throughout the process. I didn't want to leave until I could smell what was in the oven and anticipate eating it.
- **Example 2:** My mom let me help mix and pour the batter for her holiday delights when I was just 5 years old. I can still remember standing on a yellow step stool and feeling my mom's hand guide mine as we gently stirred in the flour and poured the mixture into the worn aluminum pan. I never wanted to leave before the finished product was on the counter; I wanted to stay in the kitchen to watch the oven perform its magic and smell what would soon taste so sweet.

Example 1 does not engage the listener. Example 2 allows the listener to stand with you on that "yellow step stool" and experience it all vicariously. If your audience is engaged, they will listen longer and retain more.

Sensory Secrets ideas for me

31

HANDS OF TIME

While time is not likely one of your big concerns, it will make a difference to your success as a public speaker. When you plan and practice, you need to think about how long every aspect of your program will take. If you have an activity for the audience, have you factored in someone talking more than you anticipated or the possibility of no participation? What if you give everyone a 10-minute bathroom break, and only half of the audience returns on time? What if you are a paid speaker for three hours and you finish your content with 30 minutes to fill?

Each scenario will get easier with practice and new experiences. Most importantly, never blame the audience. It is your responsibility to value their time. You will learn tricks to condense your information if you are running out of time, and you will develop a cheat sheet for questions and activities if time is standing still. Never underestimate the value of asking the audience topical questions to fill time—if you have established rapport, they will be happy to talk.

> Murphy's Law states that 'anything that can go wrong, will go wrong.' This seems to be especially true when you consider public speaking. Speaking in front of others is already a frightening experience, and when things start to go wrong during the presentation, it can become even more stressful.
>
> —Peter Khoury, Founder of Magnetic Speaking

When I was a first-year high school speech teacher, the vice principal sat in for my 6-month evaluation. I had plenty of warning and thought I had planned the class period well. I must have zoomed through the material and scared the students, who all sat stoically, not participating. I found myself with 15 minutes left before the bell rang and no idea what to do. I eyed old textbooks on a shelf and thought it would be a good idea for the students to each get one. I didn't know how old these were or what we were going to do, and as you can guess, this was a disaster. I remember apologizing to the vice principal and throwing the old textbooks away to avoid a rerun during my one-year evaluation.

Hands of Time ideas for me

32

EVERYONE SAVES FACE

There will be people who walk into your presentation late, cell phones that ring people who do not like your message or antagonize you, and event planners who forgot you requested a table up front and a projector. It's OK!

Never call people out or marginalize anyone. The speaker should demonstrate kindness and humility at all costs. Everyone is watching to see how you will respond or react. The audience may judge you harshly if you get frustrated or say something without compassion. Treat the staff helping on-site with the same respect you give to the audience—this team is doing the hard work.

> People will forget what you did, people will forget what you said, but people will never forget how you made them feel.
>
> —Maya Angelou

As I gave a welcome to a group of about 500 people, a cell phone rang from a gentleman in the front row. I took a risk and asked if I could answer the phone, and he complied. To this day, I chuckle about that conversation with his neighbor who wanted to borrow the snowplow. The audience was in stitches, and the neighbor thought I was his wife.

Everyone Saves Face ideas for me

33

PEOPLE FIRST, PROBLEM SECOND

You can make a mistake with your facts and figures, and the audience will forgive you, but it's a different story if you are unkind. We all goof up sometimes and think we say something one way, but it comes out differently, or we repeat something we thought was true, only to learn later it's false. You can recover from all this by humbly apologizing and correcting the error. Sometimes it requires a follow-up later,

> To be kind is more important than to be right. Many times, what people need is not a brilliant mind that speaks but a special heart that listens.
>
> —F. Scott Fitzgerald

which can keep you in the good books with the audience. Service recovery is still value-added customer service.

On the other hand, you can deliver your message seamlessly with subject matter expertise and supporting research. Your audience will know that you are smart and credible. But it won't matter if you are unkind to anyone in the room. Each perceived threat to an individual is a threat to the entire audience, and they will tune you out and plot revenge.

I was presenting on emotional intelligence and the clicker for the slides started to go south as it clearly needed new batteries. I had checked in with the event planner before we started, and he assured me the batteries were new. When the problems began during the presentation, I made eye contact with him, and he gave me the "sorry, but you're stuck" look. I let my frustration get the best of me as I started pushing harder on the buttons and I made a comment about new batteries. I could feel the mood in the room change as this audience watched me demonstrate a low level of emotional intelligence and embarrass myself. I left with my head hanging low and a promise to never let the problem be more important than the people.

People First, Problem Second ideas for me

34

DIRECT, HONEST, AND RESPECTFUL

There are four possible behaviors for you to exhibit when you work with people and speak to an audience: passive, passive-aggressive, aggressive, and assertive. You need to claim assertive and stick with it. Assertive means you are direct (face-to-face or directly to the person), honest (i.e., tell the truth), and respectful (it's about the situation, not the person).

You may need to remind the event planner that you requested an 8-foot table, or there might be a sidebar during your presentation that is distracting the audience. Rather than avoid these situations (passive), or complain about them with others later (passive-aggressive), or yell and get mad (aggressive), choose the assertive path to take care of them professionally. The table is a quick fix for the event planner, and the distracted audience members will appreciate you addressing the sidebar.

> Being assertive is a core communication skill.
> Assertiveness can help you express yourself effectively and stand up for your point of view. It can also help you do this while respecting the rights and beliefs of others.
>
> —Mayo Clinic on Stress Management

Passive-aggressiveness—think wolf in sheep's clothing—is the most pervasive behavior in the Western workplace. It creates distrust, hostility, and frustration. When I was in elementary school, my mom told me, "If people are talking with me about others, they are talking with others about me." Passive-aggressive people are nice to your face and talk about you behind your back. Your audience deserves direct, honest, and respectful.

Direct, Honest, and Respectful ideas for me

35

MOVE ON

Mistakes will happen during your presentation. These may include a simple word stumble or a more dramatic tumble over your computer cords. Whatever it is, acknowledge it quickly and move on with your message. The audience isn't interested in long explanations. In turn, don't start negative self-talk about the incident, either. Obsessing to yourself about what happened and worrying about it will sabotage your success.

Perhaps you experienced delayed flights and/or early morning travel woes to get to the stage, and those things are on your mind when you begin. There is no need to mention either unless the issue delayed the start of your presentation. If there is a delay, acknowledge it quickly with a simple apology and move on. You want the audience to focus on your topic, not the last 24 hours of your life.

> The key to...disarming our organic panic button is to turn the focus away from ourselves—away from whether we will mess up or whether the audience will like us—and toward helping the audience.
>
> —Sarah Gershman, "To Overcome Your Fear of Public Speaking, Stop Thinking About Yourself," *Harvard Business Review*

I was co-facilitating a workshop in Pennsylvania that was supposed to start at 9 a.m. My co-facilitator and I ended up stuck overnight in Chicago's O'Hare airport but managed to get a flight that had us at the conference center by 10 a.m. We kept the event planners up-to-date, and they were able to switch things around on the agenda. When we started, we thanked the participants and the event planners for their patience and jumped right into the workshop content. It was the audience's turn to be the focus of attention.

Move On
ideas for me

36

REAL VIRTUAL AUDIENCE

Although it is virtual when you present online, your audience is real. They are the same human beings that sit in chairs for an in-person presentation, and you must treat them with the same value and concern.

> According to a recent survey from Showpad, one in four employees (76%) say they get more distracted when on video calls vs. in-person meetings.

Pay attention to the following for your virtual presentations:

- Be the first online. The event planner should not have to wait for you.
- Remove distractions in the background and be aware of book titles, quotes, art, and memorabilia in the camera's view.
- Stand up and fill most of the screen. You wouldn't sit down in person.
- Look directly into the camera lens. It feels awkward, but it is your number one way to connect with the audience.
- Make sure you ask and permit the event planner to watch the chat box and interrupt you when appropriate if there are technical difficulties for the audience or if there is any confusion.
- Don't make negative comments if people log off or block their cameras.
- Use props and hand gestures in the camera's view to elevate the experience.
- Follow up on any chat box and Q&A questions that were not addressed during the presentation.
- Print each slide in color to hold up in case slide sharing stops working.
- Send a thank you email through the event planner to all participants.

I like to use my free-standing, brick-wall banner as a backdrop. It looks real and removes any distraction concerns. I have to get it very close to me so that the camera doesn't include anything visual outside the banner. There have been more than a few times when my audience has wondered if my "brick wall" was going to fall over when I took a sudden step back or got too animated with my hand gestures.

Real Virtual
Audience
ideas for me

37

ARE THEY AWAKE?

Just because their eyes are open doesn't mean they are awake and listening. Speakers have a responsibility to keep the audience engaged. I'm not talking about moving audience members around the room for exercise or mandating everyone volunteer for an activity.

Laughter is an indication that audience members are participating and tuned into you. No jokes are necessary here; just find opportunities to create frivolity and fun. Variety is also key. They will numb quickly with your voice and some slides, so ask questions.

> People seem to get bored after approximately 10 minutes–and it occurs in a class, lecture, or business presentation.
>
> —John Medina, Molecular biologist and author of *Brain Rules*

You may take volunteers to answer the questions in front of the whole group or instruct everyone to turn to their neighbor and discuss their responses. Be careful of sticking with the same sequence of activities. Keep them on their toes by surprising them with the order of events.

I like to tell participants, "Turn and discuss with the person to your right or left, whomever you like better." This phrase always gets a little chuckle. Before the third or fourth time of one-on-one discussions, I announce that they are welcome to change partners if they are exhausted from their first pick. I have never had anybody move, but some have probably thought about it.

Are They Awake? ideas for me

38

ASSUME NOTHING

You may think the audience member on the edge of her seat nodding "yes" is engaged and thinks you are an excellent speaker. You may also assume the person who looked at his watch, frowned and hurried out was bored or frustrated with your message. You may be correct, but there are many other explanations. The woman may need a restroom break, and the man may be late for a meeting. It is essential to pay attention to body language to watch for themes (e.g., everyone is asleep). But we can't certify our detective skills when we observe behaviors from one or two individuals.

A group of people leaving early, frowning, or sticking to their phones is a reason to pause. You need to determine if it is the content, your presentation style, or something else. It is appropriate if several people are involved to stop and ask if there is something you can do. You may learn they just received word about a corporate merger or a tragedy with a colleague. Never assume it's about you. Accept the comments and change what you can control if it is about you. It could be a simple microphone or slide issue.

> Interpret the context of your audience's body language. Don't jump to conclusions based on isolated or ambiguous signals... For example, if your audience is looking at their phones, they might not be rude or distracted. They might be taking notes, tweeting, or following your slides. Similarly, if your audience is silent, they might not be bored or confused. They might be respectful, thoughtful, or shy.
>
> —LinkedIn community article

I remember presenting about emotional intelligence to a group of about 150 staff from a community college. I observed a woman in the third row who seemed disgusted and frustrated with everything I said. I was young and inexperienced, and I thought if I looked at her more and gave more examples she would come around. None of my aggressive behavior worked, and she was the first one out the door when we finished.

Assume Nothing
ideas for me

39

ONE AND ONLY

It is tempting to reference other audiences when you are speaking. You might mention the temperature since you were with a group in Austin last week or something about the participant who shared a humorous anecdote in California. These comments seem harmless, but they can distract from the message and the unique experience for the current audience.

Audience members know that speakers meet with many people, but they also want to believe the speaker thinks of them as special and customizes the message for their specific needs. At the same time, there may be occasions when a quick reference to a different audience facing the same problems or a group that the current audience holds in high regard can help you build credibility.

I use what I call the Fabric Softener Approach. When you put a fabric softener into your laundry, it refreshes the entire load. In speaking, I rarely give a speech without trying out at least one new line or story. In doing so, that new piece becomes like the sheet of fabric softener and actually makes the entire speech fresh for me, which helps me keep it fresh for my audience. I also dedicate every speech I give to someone somewhere so that it's just as important every time I give it.

—Craig Valentine, Award-Winning Speaker & Trainer

I work with individuals to help prepare them for keynotes, plenaries, and other critical presentations. It is easy to start throwing around "this client and that client" to support a point or share an example. If I don't catch myself and stop, I can feel the energy wane in the room. No one wants to think they are just one of many or reminiscent of someone else.

One and Only
ideas for me

40

STOP

You may think your audience is on the edge of their seats listening to you, but if you go a minute over the scheduled end time, they are done listening. In fact, as the end time draws near, they are distracted and concerned you might keep talking. This rule applies to all speakers. It doesn't make a difference if you are a celebrity or promoting the local bond referendum—time matters.

> Your talks should be clear, concise, fun, exciting, and never ever run over time. For each extra minute your talk runs over, 10% more of the audience will decide you are a jerk and start fantasizing about you falling down a trap door.
>
> —John Baez, *Advice for the Young Scientist*

The best practice to maximize your audience's attention is to end five minutes early. You catch them off guard before they start worrying they will be late to their next meeting or more importantly, late for lunch. Do not try to buy yourself extra time by encroaching on the Q&A time, either. On that note, you need to end the Q&A five minutes early and let the audience know you will hang around if anybody wants to talk more.

Faculty often give me the most pushback on wrapping up five minutes early when we are preparing for a big presentation. Some are convinced that a 50-minute keynote is just a "suggestion" and believe the audience will be grateful to listen for hours.

Stop ideas for me

ENJOY
YOUR TREATS

(OUTCOME)

41

NO "GREAT QUESTION"

I cringe when I hear "great question" during a presentation Q&A. It may sound like an appropriate way to respond to an audience member, but you should think twice before you say it next time.

"Great question" is subjective. Is it great because it makes the speaker think harder, or the last question was bad, or the audience member was listening and the speaker is pleased, or is

Leadership consultant Deborah Grayson Riegel says when you're stumped in a meeting, you shouldn't say, "That's a great question." She offers three reasons why you should avoid this phrase: many times it's just a reflex, you may offend someone if you don't use it for every question, and it may not even be true.

it just a common response so the speaker can buy some time before responding? It could be any one of these or some I haven't listed. To be safe, don't say it.

Try one of the following responses instead:
- Thank you for this question.
- Yes … I mentioned something earlier that may have begged this question.
- I appreciate the question.
- Thank you.
- OK … let me know if I answer your question. I may need to follow up with you later.

No "Great
Question"
ideas for me

42

GIVE THEM THE SLIDES

I recommend you share your slides with the event planner and audience members if you receive a request. Except for proprietary information, there is more good than harm here.

Your presentation will not circulate and put you out of business. Consider it a compliment and an opportunity to build bigger and better relationships. It's important that your contact information is on a slide and that the title slide includes your name and the organization you represent.

On the topic of slide distribution, I have also given away other items that supported my program (e.g., props that connected with an individual, a clicker someone admired, and branded bags I used for my supplies). All of these items are easily replaced and giving them away may help grow my business.

> There are always three speeches, for every one you actually gave. The one you practiced, the one you gave, and the one you wish you gave.
>
> —Dale Carnegie

Early in my career, I remember recoiling when an event planner asked for my slides. I was sure that would be the end of presenting this content, and the slides would be mass-produced. I declined and never received another invitation to work with that organization again.

Give Them
the Slides
ideas for me

43

MYSTERY SHOPPER

Find yourself a mystery shopper. It is someone whose public speaking knowledge and experience you respect. You will ask them to blend into the audience for a couple of your presentations.

The feedback you get from audience members and the event planner right after you finish speaking isn't "real" feedback. Unless something goes horribly wrong, they will look you in the eye and say you did a great job. It's just the way it goes after a presentation. They want you to like them on the way out the door. Most participants who were disappointed or disagreed will type up anonymous comments when they get the email later with the feedback survey.

> Hiring a mystery shopper provides you with valuable information that can be challenging to obtain any other way. Surveys of employees and regular customers may not provide the same truth and insight as a mystery shopper who is trained to assess a customer's experience.
>
> —Indeed for Employers

You need good, honest feedback from someone who knows public speaking. Ask your mystery shopper to take notes about audience responses to anecdotes and humor. Ask them to pay attention to the overall energy in the room alongside your energy; some speakers start strong and then lose momentum. Did the mystery shopper think you exceeded expectations for the audience, or were you just status quo? Did you connect with emotion, present novel ideas, and create a memorable experience?

Do not go on the defense when you meet with your mystery shopper. This gift will take you to the next level!

When I am within 50-100 miles of a public speaking client, I beg to attend one of their events. My comments as an attendee are much more helpful than the notes I can provide when we simulate this work in a small conference room with just the two of us. I sometimes take it a step further and chat with other audience members sitting beside me. I learn a lot from those conversations, too.

Mystery Shopper ideas for me

44

TIMELY THANKS

Keep a large inventory of thank you notes to use after each speech, workshop, or presentation. Immediately after the event, you can remember specific things about individuals to include in your notes. The more customized your note, the better.

A recent *New York Times* article noted that the average household receives just 10 pieces of personal mail per year, not counting holiday cards and invitations. This makes handwritten thank-you notes significant.

You will write these notes to the event planner or the individual you worked with to make it happen, along with any individual who supported you throughout the program, including the front desk representative and the troubleshooter from IT. Beyond this, it is program-specific; if you had a small workshop with only five to seven participants, you should write a note to each person. For a large group, send a note to anyone you conversed with or who added something to the program that you remember.

No generic thank you notes. You can write down reminders about names and details at break and in the car right after you depart. Think about where you will send the notes. If you know everyone visits a central office at some point, send them all to the office.

As a child in Fairfield, Iowa, I remember my mom rushing to the post office frequently to get mail in the box by the 5 p.m. pick-up time. I was so annoyed with this when I was young. That has all changed. I always want my notes in the mail by pick-up time after my events. I will drive out of my way to find a post office or mailbox to maximize the timeliness for participants.

Timely Thanks
ideas for me

45

ONE HOUR, ONE WEEK, ONE YEAR

When you give a speech or facilitate a workshop, it qualifies as an event. Your audience may learn new information, think a bit differently, or entertain taking action. This event will only be one to three hours of their life, so what happens after is what can make the message stick!

Do you recall experiencing an elevated mood after listening to a motivational speaker or an inspiring presentation? You leave the room excited and ready to do something with the new information. But a week passes, and you are hard-pressed to remember the content or the speaker's name.

> Following up with your audience post public speaking is essential as it deepens connections and sustains engagement. This personal touch reflects your genuine interest and care, fostering trust and rapport.
>
> —Avi Wolfson, Professional public speaker

When you speak and present information, request the names and emails of the participants and follow up. Send them a PDF with additional information or a link to a value-added resource. The participants will appreciate your genuine concern for them and will re-energize involvement and action. Many public speakers stop at the performance and the applause; speakers who stay in touch will change outcomes. In addition, send something special to a participant who took a risk or was having a tough day.

I facilitated a workshop on emotional intelligence with a group of city employees. The event planner gave me a list of the participants and their jobs ahead of our time together. I noticed an employee was responsible for cleaning the park restrooms and emptying the trash. I happened to have a promotional stress ball in the shape of a porta-potty. I put it on the table where the gentleman was sitting when he was on break. He was amused when he returned to see it. After the workshop, I ordered sample stress balls in the shape of toilet paper, a toilet, and a garbage can. Imagine the employee's surprise a month after "the event" when the swag arrived in the mail. He was thrilled.

One Hour, One Week, One Year ideas for me

46

WHO IS THAT?

When you present, be kind and courteous. Demonstrate these same behaviors when you meet participants in the parking lot ahead of your talk, during the breaks, and when you see an audience member at the grocery store.

Have you ever listened to a speaker and been inspired only to meet them "off-stage" and leave you wondering where the speaker went? You may have been shocked they were rude or dismissive to a service provider or possibly yourself. This reputation will spread much faster than a reputation as a good speaker.

According to a study by Gallup, employers who engage in passive-aggressive behavior toward their employees will lead to disgruntled and disengaged workers, costing the U.S. economy up to $370 billion per year in lost productivity.

Public speaking intelligence intersects with emotional intelligence. High levels of both require you to manage yourself and your relationships positively on and off the stage.

I hired a consultant to work with my college recruitment team on public speaking and professional presence. The group thought she was the best. I remember overhearing her phone conversation on a break. This group of recruiters would have been horrified to hear what she said about them when they weren't in the room.

Who is That?
ideas for me

47

THE EXPERT IN THE ROOM

When you stand in front of an audience and ask for their time and interest, you need to be the true expert in the room. Understand your topic's history and consume knowledge about it until you present. If you share the same content about this topic that you did last year, you may have audience members who are way ahead of you.

On the flip side, be confident that you are in front of this audience because you are a subject matter expert. Anxiety is real for public speakers, but you should not be worried every one in the room

> Designing a presentation without an audience in mind is like writing a love letter and addressing it 'to whom it may concern.'
>
> —Ken Haemer, Former AT&T presentation research manager

knows more about this topic than you do. They do not. They are in those seats because they believe you have ideas, information, and insight they don't yet have. It should give you pride and calm your nerves to know you provide value to your audience.

I worked as a corporate trainer in the insurance industry. I remember being asked to clear our calendars for a morning workshop with new content from an outside company that we might consider bringing in-house. It only took a few minutes to realize this company did not do any research on its audience. We already had this program in-house, and they were humiliated when we let them know we could not waste more of their time. An audience who knows more about the topic than you do is not a friendly audience.

The Expert in the Room ideas for me

48

ULTERIOR MOTIVES

Each time you are an audience member listening to someone present from now on, you should be a public speaking student. Colleagues leading meetings and keynote speakers at national confer-
ences will provide examples of success and failure.

Make a grid and keep it handy. This grid should include a field for each key element, including content, organization, and delivery. Take it to every meeting and presentation. Did the speaker get your attention? Why

> When I think about compelling presentations, I think about taking an audience on a journey. A successful talk is a little miracle-people see the world differently afterward.
>
> —Chris Anderson, Curator of TED Talks

did the audience laugh at a certain moment? Were people nodding off? What did you remember an hour after you left? The next day? You have listened to speakers for years but probably not given much thought to the mechanics and delivery techniques. Your best teachers are right in front of you. Take advantage of this free education.

Public speaking expertise will be a blessing and a curse moving forward. It will be difficult in the future for you to suspend disbelief and focus on the content when you observe basic organization and delivery missteps. Remember, though, that everyone is doing the best with what they know. You just happen to know better, so you must DO better.

I have the opportunity to help prepare clients for keynotes, plenaries, and big interviews. I swell with pride when the client reaches out after the event to let me know participants commented on how they learned just as much from the speaker's effective public speaking skills as they learned from their content.

Ulterior Motives
ideas for me

49

MINISTERS AND TED TALKS

Ministers and TED Talk speakers are two resources to learn from quickly. Ministers who have delivered sermons for years have practiced content organization, audience analysis, effective delivery, appropriate humor, engagement, and more. No matter your religious affiliation, you can learn a lot from watching a preacher who keeps the congregation on the edge of their pews.

TED Talk speakers are some of the best. They were selected as subject matter experts and then coached to deliver their message in less than 18 minutes with a lot of wow factor. Search for them by topics or names and pay attention. Listen to the stories, watch the body language, tune into the vocal variety, and observe the reactions from the audience. What about their slides? You will notice lots of images on these slides and very little text. Also, pay attention to how the slides don't get much eye contact from the speaker. The audience takes center stage.

> One thing that helps to stretch me is to listen to other preachers' sermons. Every year, I will listen to at least ten other preachers, both to hear God speak to me and also to evaluate their preaching to see what I can learn and how I can improve my own preaching.
>
> —Pastor Adam Hamilton

Adam Hamilton, founder and senior pastor at the Church of the Resurrection in Leawood, Kansas, is a master of the message on stage. He does many hours of research to prepare for each sermon and delivers it as if he were sitting across the table from everyone in the audience. He keeps notes next to him on the pulpit for reference, but he never stands behind the pulpit. His use of relevant stories and anecdotes creates an emotional connection, and his regular use of props makes each message memorable.

50

NO BIG DEAL

It's true that good public speakers have opportunities that other subject matter experts may not get. People gravitate toward a good message with excellent delivery. You may hear loud laughs and strong applause from your audience. You may watch heads bob in agreement and receive emails on your way home for additional speaking engagements. You might even write a book.

Don't get confused by the attention. You are giving performances. You have read, listened, and practiced to improve and do your best. You have tried and failed and jumped back on stage. You have solicited honest feedback and applied it. You deserve to be recognized and appreciated, but not revered.

> I often tell coaching clients that the secret to happiness in public speaking is to let go of your ego and realize that the presentation isn't about you speaking. It's about the audience hearing something. You're in service to that audience and to the message. In the trio of speaker, message, and audience, you're the least important part.
>
> —Nick Morgan, "Don't Let Your Ego Be Your Enemy," *Forbes*

Get on the plane or in the car and remind yourself that each one of those audience members will go back to their workplace and home and struggle to remember your name tomorrow. Your kindness and empathy for others, though, will be remembered!

I admitted to my husband that I always wanted to be a "famous funny person." I'm not fit to be a stand-up comedian and I'm not reaching any celebrity status, so I will define "funny" as getting laughs on stage and "famous" as the author of this short book. Thank you for improving yourself and investing in your public speaking success. This book is about you, not me!

No Big Deal
ideas for me

ENDING NOTE

When I was 10 years old and in the fifth grade at Washington Elementary School in Fairfield, Iowa, my good friend Anna and I performed the Smothers Brothers skit, "Mom Always Liked You Best," for the annual talent show.

The laughter and applause on that day created a monster. I have never stopped trying to understand, value, and entertain the audience.

Practice makes permanent, so take these "50 Ways to Public Speaking Intelligence" and make a difference on your stage.

ACKNOWLEDGMENTS

Steve Mullan, who mentored me as a new teacher at Newton High School and never gave up.

My editor, Marin Devine, who worked magic.

Brother, Jeff, who believes his "Fatty Fiddle" label saved me.

Sons, Sam and Spencer, who laugh at me and not with me and keep me humble.

My husband, Tim, whose patience and kindness I learn from every day.

ABOUT THE AUTHOR

Stephanie Salasek has gone from high school speech teacher to stage coach working with clients in higher education, health care, start-ups, and *Fortune* 500 companies. Her clients seek her out for critical presentations that need to be remembered and make a difference.

After years of working in public education, private industry, health care, and higher education administration, Stephanie recognized the need for better speakers who could keep the audience awake and engaged.

Stephanie lives in Iowa with her husband and helps speakers "break the script" every day.

Made in the USA
Middletown, DE
25 February 2024

49919908R00066